Retirement Renaissance
Rediscovering Passion & Purpose in Later Life

ANUPAM PANDEY

BLUEROSE PUBLISHERS
India | U.K.

Copyright © Anupam Pandey 2024

All rights reserved by author. No part of this publication may be reproduced, stored in a retrieval system or transmitted in any form or by any means, electronic, mechanical, photocopying, recording or otherwise, without the prior permission of the author. Although every precaution has been taken to verify the accuracy of the information contained herein, the publisher assumes no responsibility for any errors or omissions. No liability is assumed for damages that may result from the use of information contained within.

BlueRose Publishers takes no responsibility for any damages, losses, or liabilities that may arise from the use or misuse of the information, products, or services provided in this publication.

For permissions requests or inquiries regarding this publication, please contact:

BLUEROSE PUBLISHERS
www.BlueRoseONE.com
info@bluerosepublishers.com
+91 8882 898 898
+4407342408967

ISBN: 978-93-6261-001-0

Cover Design: Sadhna Kumari
Typesetting: Pooja Sharma

First Edition: May 2024

Preface

Welcome to "Retirement Renaissance: Rediscovering Passion and Purpose in Later Life." With this book in your hand, you embark on a journey: one of discovery, inspiration and transformation as we navigate the vast landscape of retirement together.

For many people, retirement marks an important stage in life: a period of transition, reflection and renewal. It is a period that invites us to leave behind the hustle and bustle of professional life and enjoy the freedom and opportunities that await us. However, for some people, retirement can also be a source of uncertainty, anxiety and apprehension – a leap into the unknown, raising questions about identity, purpose and satisfaction.

In "Retirement Renaissance," we embark on a journey to redefine retirement, challenge the prejudices and stereotypes that often surround this stage of life and unleash true potential of our later years. We reject the notion that retirement is a time of decline and withdrawal, instead viewing it as a time of possibility and reinvention - a time to rediscover your passions, nurture your relationships by making meaningful connections and leave a lasting legacy for future generations.

But what exactly is the retirement renaissance? It's a term that captures the spirit of renewal and rebirth, celebrating the opportunities and possibilities that retirement brings. It is a call to action for retirees to embrace change with courage and curiosity, rediscover their passions and pursue them vigorously, while creating a meaningful, purposeful and satisfying life.

In "Retirement Renaissance," we will explore many of the topics and themes central to the retirement experience. Whether it's finding passion and purpose in later life, navigating financial planning and wealth management, fostering meaningful connections or embracing change with resilience and grace, we'll delve into what it means to live a fulfilling and meaningful retirement.

Throughout this book, you'll get practical advice to discover path to embark on the journeys of retirement renaissance - people who have embraced change, pursued their passions and found joy in the process as satisfaction in the later years of life. These advices serve as inspiration and guidance, providing valuable insights and lessons that we can apply to our own lives as we face the complexities of taking time off post-retirement.

"Retirement Renaissance" is a roadmap to living a vibrant, purposeful and fulfilling retirement life. This guidebook offers practical advice, concrete strategies and thought-provoking ideas to help you make the most of this precious period of your life.

Whether you approach retirement with anticipation and excitement or struggle with uncertainty and anxiety, "Retirement Renaissance" is here to support you on your journey. It is your companion, providing wisdom, encouragement and inspiration as you navigate the challenges of retirement and discover the joy and fulfilment that awaits you.

So, my dear readers, I invite you to join me on this journey: a journey of self-discovery, growth and transformation. Together, let us embrace the retirement renaissance and embark on a journey to rediscover passion and purpose later in life.

The road ahead may be uncertain, but with courage, curiosity and open hearts, we can create a truly extraordinary retirement experience, filled with joy, meaning and endless possibilities.

Welcome to "Retirement Renaissance: Rediscovering Passion and Purpose in Later Life."

Your journey begins now.

14th April 2024   **Anupam Pandey**

Acknowledgement

In the memory of my mother and younger sister, I dedicate this book.

I extend my thanks to my father, Mr. J N Pande, my wife Rashmi, my son-in-law Amarendra, my daughter Adya, my son Aditya, my daughter-in-law Diksha, my granddaughter Amaaya and my grandson Atharv, for being a moral support and enabling me to complete this book.

Also, my thanks to the Almighty without whose blessings this work would not have been possible.

Lastly my thanks to the readers of my self-help books "Frugality: Being Mindful of Your Expenses", "Time Alchemy: Transforming Moments into Success", "Grow Old Gracefully" and "Forgiveness and Healing: Letting Go of the past for a brighter future"

Introduction: Embracing the Retirement Renaissance

In the vast scope of human existence, few transitions compare to the profound change that occurs when a person enters retirement. It was the culmination of decades of whirlwind work, a time when the steady pace of routine gave way to the promise of unexplored horizons. However, for many people, this transition is about more than simply moving into a state of idleness or relaxation; it is a profound opportunity to innovate, redefine and rediscover.

Welcome to the Retirement Renaissance

In the pages that follow, we embark on a journey, one that transcends conventional notions of retirement as a period of decline. Instead, we are diving into a paradigm shift, a renaissance, where individuals are empowered to fully embrace their passions, goals and potential in later part of life. This is not a story of disconnection but a story of stepping into a new vitality, a vitality that comes not from the needs of the workforce but from the depths of each person's being.

A Change of Perspective

The Retirement Renaissance began with a fundamental shift in perspective. It challenges the outdated notion that retirement means inevitable decline – a period marked by a gradual loss of relevance and purpose. Instead, it invites us to see retirement as a threshold, a gateway to a new chapter full of promise, possibility and profound personal growth. In this renaissance, age is not a limitation but a badge of honour - a testament to wisdom gained, life experienced and lessons learned. It is a time when individuals feel liberated from the constraints of societal expectations, free to chart their own paths and define success on their own terms. It is a time to honour the past, fully embrace the present and embrace the future with open arms.

Rediscover Your Passion

The focus of Retirement Renaissance is pursuing passion. Freed from the demands of daily life, retirees have the opportunity to reconnect with long-forgotten hobbies, interests and dreams. Whether painting, gardening, photography or music, retreats provide the space and time to explore the depths of creativity and self-expression. But passion goes beyond individual activities: it includes the joy of learning, the thrill of adventure and the satisfaction of making a difference in the lives of others. Whether it's signing up for a cooking class or volunteering at a local shelter, retirees have the opportunity to give purpose and meaning to each moment, igniting the fire within. The day burns more and more with each passing day.

Accept a Goal

However, the Retirement Renaissance is not just about enjoying personal pleasures but also about finding purpose in every aspect of life. Whether through meaningful work, volunteerism or acts of kindness, retirees have the ability to make a lasting impact on the world around them. This is the time to leverage the skills and experience accumulated for the common good, mentor the next generation and leave a legacy that will transcend the limits of time.

But purpose isn't just found in external endeavours: it's also cultivated through introspection, self-discovery and the pursuit of personal growth. It's about embracing the journey of discovery, embracing the journey of becoming the best version of yourself and thriving in the simple joys of everyday life.

A Holistic Approach to Happiness

At the heart of the Retirement Renaissance is the recognition that true fulfilment goes beyond material wealth or career accolades. It encompasses total wellness of mind, body and spirit – a harmony that needs to be nurtured with intention and care. From staying active and engaged to practicing mindfulness and self-care, retirees have the opportunity to prioritize their health and happiness in ways that were previously unimaginable.

But perhaps most importantly, Retirement Renaissance invites us to nurture meaningful connections - with loved ones, with community and with the natural world. Through these connections, we find comfort, support and a sense of belonging, a reminder that we are never truly alone on this journey called life.

Conclusion: A Journey of Renewal

As we begin our journey through the Retirement Renaissance, let's embrace the limitless possibilities that await us. Let us cast off the shackles of outdated expectations and embrace the freedom to live authentically, passionately and with purpose. For in the twilight years, we discover not an end but a new beginning: a rebirth of the soul, illuminating the path to a truly good life.

Contents

Part I: Understanding Retirement Renaissance 1

Part II: Rediscovering Passion 13

Part III: Finding Purpose 25

Part IV: Wellness and Well-being 39

Part V: Navigating Relationships and Nurturing the Soul 53

Part VI: Financial Freedom and Security 67

About the Author 81

Disclaimer 84

Part I:
Understanding Retirement Renaissance

In the journey towards retirement, there is a profound opportunity for transformation: the chance to embrace a new era of vitality, purpose and fulfilment. However, to fully grasp the nature of this transition, one must first understand the fundamentals of the Retirement Renaissance. In this section, we delve into the heart of this paradigm shift, exploring its origins, significance and profound potential to reshape the future landscape of life.

The Evolution of Retirement

To understand the Retirement Renaissance, it is essential to think about the evolution of retirement itself. Traditionally considered a time of rest and relaxation, retirement once meant retiring from the workforce: a time to reap the rewards of a lifetime of work and settle into a life of well-deserved rest.

However, as societal norms and expectations evolve, so does the concept of retirement. No longer content to take a back seat, today's retirees are redefining what it means to "retire." They rejected the notion of leisure in favour of active engagement, seeking not only relaxation but also a renewed sense of purpose and passion in later life.

New Paradigm

At the heart of the Retirement Renaissance is a new paradigm: a shift in thinking that challenges traditional narratives about old age and retirement. Instead of viewing late life as a period of decline, this model celebrates the potential for growth, passion and self-discovery.

In this new paradigm, age is not a barrier but a gateway: a gateway to new experiences, new connections and new opportunities. It is a time when individuals are freed from the pressure of social expectations, free to chart their own path and pursue their passions with relentless enthusiasm.

Accept Change

At the heart of the Retirement Renaissance is the recognition that change is not only inevitable but necessary for growth. As retirees navigate the transition from the workforce to retirement, they face countless choices and challenges. Yet it is in these moments of uncertainty that the seeds of transformation are sown.

Accepting change requires a willingness to let go of the familiar and embrace the unknown, venturing beyond the boundaries of one's comfort zone in search of new horizons. It is a journey marked by resilience, adaptability and an ongoing commitment to self-discovery.

Navigating Transitions Later in Life

The transition to retirement is not a one-time event but a series of ongoing adjustments - a continuous process of adaptation and evolution. From the initial excitement of newfound freedom to the gradual adjustment to daily life, retirees must navigate a complex range of emotions and experiences.

However, these transformations have opportunities for growth and innovation. It is an opportunity to let go of the constraints of the past and embrace the possibilities of the future, rewrite the script of one's life and embark on a journey of self-discovery and reinvention.

Conclusion: Embrace the Journey

As we embark on an exploration of the Retirement Renaissance, let us embrace the profound potential that lies within each of us. Let us set aside the limitations of the past and embrace the limitless possibilities of the future. For amid change and uncertainty, we discover not just an ending but a new beginning: a rebirth of spirit that illuminates the path to a truly good life.

The Evolution of Retirement: From Rest to Renewal

Retirement, as a concept, has taken a fascinating journey through history. What began as a pipe dream for many has become a fundamental aspect of modern life: a period marked not only by rest but also by renewal, reinvention and regeneration. In this journey through the evolution of retirement, we explore its origins, trace its transformation over time and illuminate the path to a dynamic new era of life.

Origins of Retirement

The concept of retirement, in its earliest forms, originated in ancient civilizations. For example, in ancient Rome, soldiers received pensions after many years of service, giving them financial security in their later years. Similarly, in ancient China, civil servants were allowed to retire at a certain age, with pensions and land grants to support them in old age.

However, it was not until the late 19th and early 20th centuries that retirement began to take shape as a social institution. The industrial revolution was accompanied by longer life spans and increased productivity, leading to the emergence of a clear division between work and leisure. As unions fight for better working conditions and shorter working hours, retirement has become a tangible goal for many workers: a final chance to enjoy the fruits of their labour after many years of hardship.

Rest Period

In the early days, retirement was primarily seen as a time of rest and relaxation, a well-deserved break after a hardworking life. For many people, the transition from the workforce to retirement is greeted with a sense of relief, offering the opportunity to escape the demands of daily life and enjoy a slower pace of life. At that time, retirement often meant relaxation. Many retirees spend their days pursuing their hobbies, traveling, or simply enjoying simple pleasures of relaxation.

While this period of rest is certainly important for recovery and relaxation, it often lacks meaning or direction beyond stopping work.

Towards Innovation

However, in recent decades, retirement has undergone a significant transformation: the shift from rest to renewal. As life expectancy continues to increase and attitudes toward aging evolve, retirees increasingly seek opportunities for personal growth, fulfilment and self-discovery later in life. This change is driven by a variety of factors, including changing social norms, advances in health care and technology and growing awareness of the importance of mental health, spirit and emotions.

However, as the baby boomer generation reaches retirement age, there is a common desire to redefine what it means to "retire": to move beyond traditional notions of leisure and enjoyment and a more comprehensive future life.

Accept Renewal in Retirement

Today, retirement is no longer considered a static destination but a dynamic journey: an opportunity to discover new passions, pursue long-held dreams and make meaningful contributions to society. Whether through volunteering, lifelong learning or entrepreneurship, retirees have opportunities for personal and professional growth far beyond the confines of the workplace.

Additionally, retirement brings the freedom to prioritize happiness in all its forms, focusing on physical health, mental sharpness and emotional fulfilment. From staying active and engaged to maintaining social connections and cultivating a sense of purpose, retirees are redefining what it means to age with grace and vitality.

Conclusion

In short, the evolution of retirement – from rest to renewal – reflects a broader shift in societal attitudes towards aging and the end of life. What was once considered a time of retreat and decline is now seen as a time of opportunity, growth and discovery. As we continue to face the complexities of retirement in the 21st century, let's embrace the possibilities that await us and rediscover passion and purpose at every stage of life.

The New Paradigm: Shifting Perspectives on Aging

In the tapestry of human existence, few threads are as tightly woven as our perception of aging. For centuries, the passage of time has been synonymous with decline – gradually fading into oblivion as the years inevitably pass. However, at the dawn of the 21st century, a seismic shift is taking place: a paradigm shift that challenges entrenched narratives about aging and redefines what it means to be old. In exploring this new paradigm of aging, we delve deeper into changing attitudes toward the end of life, highlight the transformative power of perspective, and chart a path toward a future hybrid in which age is not a limit but a source of strength, wisdom and vitality.

Old Story

For generations, aging has been saddled with countless stereotypes and stigmas – a cultural narrative that equates aging with a decline in value, relevance and worth. From literary and media representations to social expectations and institutional practices, the dominant message is clear: youth is valued, while age is marginalized. This popular narrative of decline has profound implications for individuals as they navigate the aging journey. This can erode self-esteem, weaken confidence and reduce feelings of purpose and belonging. Additionally, it can perpetuate ageism, a form of discrimination that marginalizes older people and perpetuates harmful stereotypes about their abilities and contributions.

The Emergence of a New Model

Yet amid outdated beliefs, a new paradigm of aging is emerging: one rooted in the empowerment, capabilities and inherent dignity of each individual, regardless of age. At its core is a fundamental change in perspective: the realization that old age is not an obstacle to be overcome but a journey to be undertaken - a journey rich in opportunities for growth, exploration and self-discovery.

This new paradigm is driven by a variety of factors, including advances in health care and technology, changing social norms and attitudes toward aging and the growing impact growth of the baby boomer generation- means growing old with grace and vitality.

Redefining Aging

At the heart of the new aging paradigm is the recognition that chronological age does not determine a person's worth or potential. Rather than focusing on the limitations imposed by the passage of time, this model emphasizes possibilities – the opportunities for personal growth, improvement and contribution that come with each stage of life.

In this model, aging is depicted as a journey of self-discovery and renewal – an opportunity to discover new passions, pursue long-held dreams and establish meaningful connections with others. This is the time to prioritize wellness in all its forms, nourish the body, mind, spirit and cultivate a sense of purpose that transcends the boundaries of age.

Embracing Diversity

Additionally, the new aging paradigm celebrates the diversity of aging experiences – a recognition that no two individuals are alike and that each person has unique talents, experiences and perspectives. It challenges the homogenizing tendency of ageism and celebrates the richness and complexity of later life in its myriad forms. From the vibrant energy of active retirees to the quiet wisdom of older adults, every stage of aging is appreciated and honoured in this model. It is a celebration of the vast tapestry of human existence, a recognition that age is just one thread in life's fabric, woven with countless others to create a masterpiece of resilience, strength and beauty.

Conclusion

In short, the new aging paradigm offers a glimmer of hope in a world haunted by aging - a vision of later life characterized by possibility, purpose and potential. As we continue to address the complexities of aging in the 21st century, let us embrace this paradigm shift with open hearts, minds and together create a future in that age is not a barrier but a source of change, inspiration and empowerment.

Embracing Change: Navigating Transitions in Later Life

Life is a journey of constant change – a series of transitions that shape our experiences, our identities and our paths forward. Nowhere is this more evident than in the transition to old age, where the context of retirement offers both challenges and opportunities for growth, innovation and self-discovery. In our exploration of embracing change and navigating later life transitions, we delve into the complexities of retirement, shed light on the transformative power of adaptation and outline the path towards a future, purpose and possibility filled with passion.

Motivation for Retirement

Retirement marks an important transition in an individual's life: a significant shift from structured routines to the uncharted territory of leisure and autonomy. For many people, this transition comes with a mix of emotions: excitement over newfound freedom, uncertainty about the future and maybe even a feeling of losing the rhythm of work.

Navigating these dynamics requires a willingness to embrace change, let go of the past and seize the opportunities available to us. It is a journey of self-discovery and renewal, an opportunity to redefine one's sense of identity, purpose and fulfilment later in life.

The power of adaptation: Adaptability, or the ability to respond flexibly and creatively to challenges and opportunities that arise along the way, is essential to accepting change later in life. This requires a resilient, open and curious mindset, willing to step out of one's comfort zone and explore new horizons.

Adjusting to retirement may involve exploring new hobbies and interests, establishing new social connections, or seeking opportunities for continued education and personal growth. It can also involve re-evaluating one's priorities, values and making intentional choices that align with one's purpose and well-being.

Handling Transitions

However, managing transitions later in life is not always easy. Retirement can bring a sense of loss – for the structure and identity work once created, for the social connections formed in the workplace and for the sense of purpose that comes from contributing to the larger community. Dealing with these transitions requires compassion, patience and care.

It's important to allow yourself the space to grieve what's been lost, while also enjoying the opportunities for growth and renewal that retirement brings. Seeking support from friends, family or professional counsellors can be invaluable in navigating the complex emotions of this transition and finding a sense of balance and fulfilment later in life.

Create a vision for the future: Ultimately, embracing change later in life is about creating a vision for the future, based on authenticity, purpose and meaning. This may involve setting new goals and aspirations, redefining your sense of identity and self-worth and cultivating a sense of gratitude and acceptance for the opportunities that retirement brings.

Creating a vision for the future also requires a willingness to be flexible and adaptive, to recognize that life is an ever-changing journey and that change is an inevitable and essential part of the process. By embracing change with open hearts and minds, retirees can navigate future life transitions with grace, resilience and a sense of possibility.

Conclusion

In short, accepting change and managing transitions later in life is a profound journey, filled with challenges, opportunities and thoughtful moments of growth and transformation. By embracing the power of adaptation, managing transitions with compassion resilience and creating a vision for the future grounded in authenticity and purpose, retirees can chart a path toward a future filled with passion, purpose and possibility.

Part II:
Rediscovering Passion

Retirement isn't just about leaving the workforce; It is about entering a new chapter of life with many opportunities for exploration, growth and self-discovery. In "Rediscovering Passion," the second part of our journey through the Retirement Renaissance, we explore the profound potential of retirement to rekindle passion, pursue long-held dreams and foster a sense of fulfilment that transcends the boundaries of work.

Find Your Passion

Central to finding your passion in retirement is discovering hobbies, interests and activities that bring joy and fulfilment. For many people, work demands may have overshadowed these passions over the years, leaving them dormant or forgotten.

Retirement offers the freedom to rediscover these passions, reconnecting with activities and experiences that bring a sense of vitality and purpose to life. Whether it's gardening, painting, cooking or playing music, retirees have the opportunity to immerse themselves in activities that nourish the soul and spark the imagination. By pursuing these passions, retirees can tap into a source of creativity, joy and fulfilment that brings meaning and purpose to every aspect of their lives.

Creative Activities

When retiring, the creative spirit flourishes, freed from the constraints of time or obligations. Many retirees find themselves drawn to artistic activities, whether painting, writing, photography or crafts, as a means of expression and exploration. These creative endeavours provide a platform for self-discovery and reflection, allowing retirees to express themselves authentically and share their unique perspectives with the world.

Additionally, the creative process itself can be deeply satisfying, providing a sense of flow and integration, bringing individuals into higher states of awareness and presence. Whether capturing the beauty of nature through a camera lens or conveying emotions on a canvas, creative pursuits in retirement offer limitless avenues for self-expression and personal growth.

The Joy of Learning

Retirement is also a time for lifelong learning: broadening horizons, acquiring new skills and delving deeper into topics of interest that may have been neglected during the busy years of one's career.

Whether it's enrolling in classes at a local community college, participating in workshops and seminars, or pursuing independent research, retirees have plenty of opportunities to raise money and nurture their curiosity and stimulate their mind.

Additionally, continued lifelong learning in retirement offers benefits that go beyond intellectual stimulation. It promotes feelings of growth and development, keeps the mind sharp and engaged and opens the door to new experiences and connections. By embracing the joy of learning in retirement, individuals can foster a sense of vitality and curiosity that enriches every aspect of their lives.

Conclusion

In short, "Rediscovering Passion" is a celebration of the limitless potential of retirement to ignite passion, pursue creative endeavours and embrace the joy of lifelong learning. By exploring life-long interests, exploring creative pursuits and embracing the joy of learning, retirees can access sources of vitality, purpose and fulfilment that bring meaning and fulfilment for every moment of their lives over the years. In the Retirement Renaissance, the journey to rediscovering passion isn't just about rediscovering lost hobbies; it is about embracing the fullness of life and discovering new paths of growth, expression and self-discovery.

Unearthing Your Passions: Exploring Hobbies and Interests

Retirement marks an important transition in life: a time to pause, reflect and rediscover passions that may have fallen dormant during the hustle and bustle of working years. In this chapter, "Unearthing Your Passions," we explore the profound potential of retirement to connect individuals with activities, hobbies and interests that bring joy, fulfilment and purpose for their lives. From gardening to painting, cooking to music, the retreat provides a canvas for expression, discovery and personal growth like no other.

The Importance of Hobbies and Interests

Hobbies and interests are more than just pastimes: they are windows to the soul, reflect our unique personalities and are a source of joy and satisfaction. However, with the demands of professional and family life, these passions can often take a back seat, pushed to the sidelines of our busy schedules. Retirement offers the opportunity to reclaim these passions and prioritize self-care, exploration and creative expression in ways that may have been neglected in the past.

Additionally, hobbies and interests play an important role in maintaining mental and emotional health in retirement. They provide a sense of structure and purpose, combat feelings of isolation and loneliness and provide a source of satisfaction and pride in one's achievements. By exploring these passions in retirement, individuals can tap into a source of vitality and meaning that infuses joy and purpose into every aspect of their later years.

Explore the Possibilities

The beauty of retirement is freedom: the freedom to explore new interests, try new activities and pursue passions that may have been put on the back burner during your working years. Whether it's gardening, carpentry, photography or bird watching, retirees have the opportunity to immerse themselves in activities that bring them joy and satisfaction. Exploring the possibilities of hobbies and interests in retirement isn't just about trying new things: it's about discovering what truly lights your soul, what brings a sense of vitality and excitement.

It's about embracing the adventure of self-discovery and allowing yourself the space to pursue your curiosity and explore new avenues of expression and creativity.

Fuel Your Passion

Once you've discovered your passions in retirement, the next step is to nurture and cultivate them, making room in your life for the activities and pursuits that bring you joy and fulfilment. This could mean devoting time every day to your hobbies, making space in your home for creative expression, or connecting with people who share your interests.

Nurturing your passion in retirement is about more than just indulging in recreational activities, it's about investing in yourself, prioritizing self-care and celebrating the things that bring you joy and fulfilment.

By making time for your passions, you not only enrich your own life but also contribute to the happiness of those around you, infusing every interaction with a sense of vitality and meaning.

Conclusion

In short, "Unearthing Your Passions" is a celebration of retirement's limitless potential to connect individuals with activities, hobbies and interests that bring joy, satisfaction and purpose for their lives. By exploring possibilities, nurturing your passions and prioritizing self-care and creative expression, retirees can tap into a source of vitality and meaning that permeates every aspect of their lives, filling their later years with joy, satisfaction and purpose. In the Retirement Renaissance, the journey to discovering your passion is not just about rediscovering lost hobbies or interests, but also about embracing life to the fullest and discovering new avenues for growth.

Creative Pursuits: Tapping into Artistic Expression

Retirement is a time of liberation, a chance to escape the constraints of the working world and embrace the freedom to explore new avenues of self-expression and creativity. In this "Creative Pursuits" chapter, we dive deeper into the transformative power of artistic expression in later life, exploring how retirees can tap into their creative potential to enrich your life and rediscover a sense of passion and purpose.

The Power of Artistic Expression

Artistic expression is a universal language: a means of communicating thoughts, feelings and experiences in a way that transcends words and boundaries. Whether painting, writing, sculpting or dancing, creative pursuits offer limitless avenues for self-discovery, healing and personal growth. For retirees, artistic expression is especially powerful: it offers a way to rediscover lost passions, discover new interests and foster a sense of vitality and purpose later in life.

Whether you are an experienced artist or a beginner, the retreat gives you the freedom and opportunity to immerse yourself in the creative process and unleash your inner artist.

Explore the Creative Process

The beauty of artistic expression lies not only in the finished product but also in the journey: the process of creation, exploration and discovery. In retirement, retirees have the opportunity to devote time to their creative pursuits, allowing them to fully immerse themselves in the creative process and explore new techniques, styles and mediums. Whether you paint a landscape, write a poem or make a piece of pottery, the creative process offers an opportunity to connect with your deepest thoughts and feelings, expressing yourself authentically and understand the chaos of life.

Additionally, the act of creation itself can be deeply satisfying, providing a sense of flow and immersion that transports you to higher states of awareness and presence.

Meet Creative Challenges

In retirement, it is important to accept creative challenges, step out of your comfort zone and explore new horizons. Whether experimenting with a new artistic medium, approaching a complex artistic technique, or collaborating with other artists, challenges provide opportunities for personal growth, learning and development.

Additionally, overcoming creative challenges in retirement can be very rewarding: it builds confidence, resilience and a sense of accomplishment that permeates every aspect of life. By facing challenges with open hearts and minds, retirees can tap into their full creative potential and open new avenues of expression and discovery.

Promote Creative Community

Finally, retirement offers the opportunity to cultivate a creative community: a network of like-minded people who share your passion for artistic expression and support your creative journey. Whether it's taking a local art class, attending workshops and seminars, or participating in online forums and communities, connecting with people who share your interests can be invaluable in nurturing your creative spirit and inspiring you to new heights of artistic expression.

Additionally, a creative community provides a sense of belonging, camaraderie and mutual support that enhances the creative process and enriches every aspect of retirement living. By surrounding yourself with other artists and creatives, you not only expand your artistic horizons: you also build a network of friends and allies who share your passion for creativity and self-expression.

Conclusion

In short, "Creative Pursuits" is a celebration of the transformative power of artistic expression later in life. Whether you draw, write, sculpt or dance, retirement gives you the freedom and opportunity to tap into your creative potential and rediscover a sense of passion and determination that helps every aspect of your life. Your life is imbued with joy, vitality and meaning. During the Retirement Renaissance, the creative pursuit was not just about creating art but also about embracing the fullness of life, connecting with the deepest self and discovering new paths to develop, explore and express yourself.

The Joy of Learning: Lifelong Education and Personal Growth

Retirement marks a new chapter in life: the opportunity to explore, develop and pursue your passions with a new sense of freedom and curiosity. In this chapter, "The Joy of

Learning," we dive deeper into the transformative power of continuing education later in life, exploring how retirees can use the joy of learning to enrich their lives, expand their horizons and rediscover a sense of passion and purpose.

Apply Lifelong Education

Lifelong learning is more than just a hobby: it is a mindset, a philosophy and a path to personal growth and fulfilment. In retirement, retirees have the opportunity to engage in continuing education in all its forms: engaging in formal research, informal exploration and self-directed learning to nourish the mind, body and spirit. Whether it's enrolling in classes at a local community college, participating in seminars and workshops or pursuing independent research, retirement offers countless opportunities to broaden your horizons, learn new skills and explore topics of interest that may have been overlooked during busy times of the years of his/her career.

Additionally, continuing education in retirement offers benefits beyond intellectual stimulation: it promotes a sense of growth and development, keeps the mind sharp and engaged and opens the door to new experiences and connections.

The Joy of Discovery

One of the greatest joys of lifelong learning is the joy of discovery: the joy of discovering new ideas, perspectives and knowledge that challenge assumptions and expand horizons. In retirement, retirees can spend time delving deeper into topics they care about, exploring new avenues of knowledge and engaging with ideas and concepts that spark curiosity and their passion. Whether it's studying art, history, learning a new language, or discovering the wonders of science, the joys of discovery in retirement are endless.

From visiting museums and libraries to attending lectures and discussions, retirees have a wealth of resources at their fingertips to support them on their lifelong learning journey and inspire them to reach new heights of intellectual and personal development.

Foster Connection and Community

Additionally, lifelong learning in retirement offers the opportunity to foster connection and community - a network of like-minded people who share your passion for learning and support your wisdom journey. Whether it's joining a book club, attending a lecture series, or participating in online forums and discussion groups, connecting with people who share your interests can be invaluable for nurturing a love of learning and inspires you to attain new heights of intellectual and self-development.

Moreover, a sense of camaraderie, belonging and mutual support enhances the learning process and enriches every aspect of retirement life. By surrounding yourself with other learners and educators, you not only expand your intellectual horizons: you also build a community of friends and allies who share a passion for lifelong learning and personal development.

Mastery Achievements

Finally, lifelong learning in retirement provides the opportunity to pursue mastery - a deep understanding and mastery of topics of interest that provide a sense of satisfaction and accomplishment. Whether mastering a new skill, perfecting a craft, or delving deeper into a field, pursuing mastery in retirement provides benefits beyond intellectual stimulation: it fosters a sense of accomplishment. Achievement, pride and satisfaction enrich every aspect of life.

Also, the process of mastering new skills and knowledge in retirement can be very rewarding: it builds confidence, resilience and infuses a sense of achievement in every aspect of life. By embracing the joy of learning in retirement, retirees can tap into the wellspring of vitality, purpose and fulfilment that gives meaning and significance to every moment of their later years.

Conclusion

In short, "The Joy of Learning" is a celebration of the transformative power of continuing education later in life. Whether you're exploring new subjects, connecting with other learners or pursuing mastery in a field, retirement offers the opportunity to enjoy the joys of learning in all its forms and rediscover. A sense of purpose, passion and determination permeates every aspect of your life with joy, vitality and meaning. In the Retirement Renaissance, the journey of lifelong learning is not just about acquiring knowledge but also about embracing the fullness of life, expanding horizons and discovering new paths to growth, explore and discover yourself.

Part III:
Finding Purpose

Retirement is not just a time to relax and enjoy the fruits of your labour; It's a tremendous opportunity to rediscover a sense of purpose, a chance to engage with the world in meaningful ways, contribute to important goals and leave a lasting legacy for future generations.

In this part of "Finding Purpose," we explore the transformative power of purpose in later life, illustrating how retirees can harness their passions and talents for positive impact, engage with the world around them and find satisfaction beyond the boundaries of work.

The Search for Purpose

At the heart of the retirement journey is the search for purpose, a deep desire to find meaning and purpose in one's later years. For many people, the transition from work to retirement can be accompanied by feelings of uncertainty and existential questions: what's next? What are my goals now that I'm no longer working? However, retirement offers a unique opportunity to explore new avenues for purpose and fulfilment, discovering passions, talents and interests that may have been overlooked during busy years in one's career.

Whether it's volunteering, mentoring or pursuing creative activities, retirees have the freedom and opportunity to make a meaningful difference in the world around them and leave a lasting legacy for future generations.

Make Differences

One of the most effective ways to find purpose in retirement is to make a difference: by contributing to the problem, advocating for positive change and making the world better than it already is.

Whether it's volunteering at a local charity, working with disadvantaged youth or advocating for environmental protection, retirees have opportunities to use their time, resources and their abilities to have a positive impact on the world around them.

Also, making a difference in retirement has benefits beyond the tangible impact: it fosters a sense of fulfilment, pride and satisfaction that enriches every aspect of life. By contributing to that important problem, retirees can tap into a sense of purpose and meaning that instils joy, vitality and meaning in every moment of their later years.

Pursue your Passion with Purpose

Another effective way to find purpose in retirement is to pursue your passions with resolve, engaging in activities and pursuits that bring joy and fulfilment while also serving those in need. Whether it's using their artistic talents to raise awareness about social issues, mentoring youth in your community, or starting a business that benefits the community, retirees have the opportunity to align their passions with their values and have a positive impact on the world around them.

What's more, pursuing passion with purpose has benefits beyond personal satisfaction: it fosters a sense of connection, belonging and contribution that enriches every aspect of life. By aligning their passion with their purpose, retirees can tap into a sense of meaning and importance that instils purpose, passion and fulfilment in every moment of their lives.

Leave a Lasting Legacy

Ultimately, retirement offers the opportunity to leave a lasting legacy, a testament to your impact on the world and the lives you've touched along the way. Whether through philanthropy, mentoring or creative expression, retirees have the opportunity to leave a legacy that will endure for generations to come: a legacy of love, compassion and positive change.

Additionally, leaving a lasting legacy in retirement offers benefits beyond personal satisfaction: it fosters a sense of immortality, knowing that your contributions will live on long for ever. By leaving a lasting legacy, retirees can tap into a sense of purpose and significance that transcends boundaries of time and space, leaving a mark on the world that will last for many years to come for future generations.

Conclusion

In short, "Finding Purpose" is a celebration of the transformative power of purpose in later life. Whether you are making a difference, pursuing a passion with purpose or leaving a lasting legacy, retirement offers the opportunity to tap into meaning and purpose that infuses joy, vitality and meaning into every aspect of your life. In the Retirement Renaissance, finding purpose is not just about personal fulfilment, but about making a positive impact on the world and leaving a lasting legacy that will last for generations to come.

Reimagining Work: Entrepreneurship and Encore Careers

Retirement is no longer just a destination: it's a journey filled with opportunities for reinvention, discovery and new beginnings. In this chapter, "Reimagining Work," we explore the transformative potential of entrepreneurship and new careers later in life, exploring how retirees can capitalize on the skills, experience and passion to create meaningful work that brings joy, purpose and fulfilment.

The Rise of Entrepreneurship

Entrepreneurship is on the rise among retirees, driven by a combination of factors including longer life expectancies, changing attitudes towards aging and technological advances that have made establishing and managing a business much easier than ever. In retirement, individuals have the opportunity to turn their passions into profit, pursue new business ventures and create a legacy that goes beyond the limits of the traditional workforce.

Additionally, entrepreneurship gives retirees the freedom and flexibility to design their own work schedules, pursue projects that align with their values and interests and take ownership of their destiny. Whether starting a small business, freelancing or consulting, retirees have the opportunity to reinvent work on their own terms and create a career that brings them joy, purpose and satisfaction in later life.

The Power of Encore Career

Encore careers, or second acts later in life, give retirees the opportunity to move into new fields, explore new interests and make a significant impact on the world around them. Whether transitioning from a corporate career to a nonprofit, pursuing a passion project or embarking on a new career path, retirees have the opportunity to utilize their skills, experience and their wisdom to create positive change in the world.

In addition, encore careers offer benefits beyond personal fulfilment: they provide opportunities for continuous learning and development, foster connections and provide a sense of purpose and meaning that transcends the work boundaries. By adopting a new career in retirement, individuals can tap into a sense of vitality and purpose that fills every aspect of their later years with joy, passion and fulfilment.

Take the Challenge

While entrepreneurship and career advancement offer tremendous opportunities for innovation and personal growth later in life, they are not without challenges. Whether it's financial considerations or the complexities of starting a new business, retirees can encounter obstacles along the way that require resilience, determination and ingenuity to overcome.

Additionally, the transition from the workforce to a startup or a new career can be difficult, requiring retirees to navigate a steep learning curve and adapt to new roles and responsibilities. However, with perseverance, creativity and a willingness to embrace the unknown, retirees can overcome these challenges and create a professional retirement life that brings them joy, purpose and success.

Building a Legacy

One of the most powerful aspects of a business career and retirement is the opportunity to build a legacy, a testament to your impact on the world and the lives you've touched along the way. Whether creating jobs, supporting charitable causes or finding innovative solutions to pressing social challenges, retirees have the opportunity to leave a legacy that will last for generations.

Moreover, building a legacy in retirement offers benefits beyond personal satisfaction: it fosters a sense of immortality, knowing that your contributions will live on for ever. By building a legacy through entrepreneurship and new careers, retirees can tap into a sense of purpose and significance that transcends the boundaries of time and space, leaving a mark on the world. The world will exist for many generations to come.

Conclusion

In short, "Reimagining Work" is a celebration of the transformative potential of entrepreneurship and new careers later in life. Whether you're starting a new business, pursuing a passion project, or embarking on a second job in a new career field, retirement offers the opportunity to reimagine work in a new way of your own and create a career that brings joy, purpose and fulfilment. In the Retirement Renaissance, creative work is about more than just making a living: it's about creating a legacy, leaving a mark on the world and embracing life to the fullest on every step of the way.

Volunteerism and Giving Back: Finding Fulfilment in Service

Retirement marks a new chapter in life: a time to reflect, reassess and rediscover what's truly important. In this chapter, "Volunteerism and Giving Back," we explore the profound potential of service and philanthropy later in life, shedding light on how retirees can find fulfilment, purpose and meaning by giving back to their community and having a positive impact on the world around them.

Strength of Service

Service is a powerful force for good: a way to connect with others, build community and create positive change in the world. In retirement, individuals have the opportunity to use their time, talents and resources to serve causes they care about, whether that is volunteering with a local charity, supporting a non-profit organization or advocate for social justice and equality.

Additionally, this service provides benefits beyond the tangible impact: it fosters a sense of connection, belonging and purpose that enriches every aspect of life. By giving back to their communities, retirees can enjoy a sense of fulfilment and satisfaction that transcends the boundaries of work and brings joy and meaning to their later years.

Find the Right Solution

One of the keys to growing in service is finding the right people: a cause or organization that matches your values, interests and talents. Whether it's working with children, supporting environmental conservation, or helping those in need, retirees have many opportunities to get involved and make a difference in areas that matter to them and how it affects them personally.

Additionally, finding the right people in the department isn't just about finding a cause: it's about finding a purpose and a sense of belonging in the work they do. By connecting with like-minded people and organizations who share their passion for service, retirees can build meaningful relationships and create lasting bonds that help enriching every aspect of their lives.

The Joy of Giving

Giving doesn't just mean making a difference: it's also about experiencing the joy of giving, the feeling of fulfilment and satisfaction that comes from knowing that you've made a positive impact on someone else's life.

Whether it's donating your time, money, or lending your expertise to a cause, giving back in retirement has immeasurable benefits: it nourishes the soul, strengthens the mind and promotes feelings of connection and compassion that enrich every aspect of life.

Additionally, giving back in retirement provides benefits beyond personal satisfaction: it fosters a sense of connection, belonging and purpose that transcends the boundaries of work and brings joy and meaning to every moment. By giving back to their communities, retirees can enjoy a sense of fulfilment and satisfaction, making every aspect of their later years full of meaning, passion and value.

Leave a Lasting Legacy

Ultimately, giving back in retirement offers the opportunity to leave a lasting legacy, a testament to your impact on the world and the lives you've touched along the way. Whether through philanthropy, volunteerism, or advocacy, retirees have the opportunity to leave a legacy that will last for generations to come: a legacy of love, kindness and compassion and positive change.

Moreover, leaving a lasting legacy in retirement offers benefits beyond personal satisfaction: it fosters a sense of immortality, knowing that your contributions will live on for ever. By giving back to their communities, retirees can tap into a sense of purpose and significance that transcends boundaries of time and space, leaving a mark on the world that will last for many years to come.

Conclusion

In short, "Volunteerism and Giving Back" is a celebration of the transformative potential of service and philanthropy later in life. Whether you volunteer, donate money, or lend your expertise to a cause, retirement offers the opportunity to give back to your community and make a positive impact to the world around you. In the Retirement Renaissance, giving isn't just about making a difference: it's also about finding fulfilment, purpose and meaning by serving others and leaving a lasting legacy for future generations.

Legacy Building: Leaving a Lasting Impact

Retirement is not just the end; it's about leaving a mark on the world, a legacy that lives on long after we're gone. In this "Legacy Building" chapter, we explore retirement's profound potential to create lasting impact, shedding light on how retirees can leverage their time, talents and resources, to leave a legacy for someone else's future and upcoming generations.

Determine Inheritance

What is inheritance? It is more than the sum of our achievements or the wealth we leave behind: it is the mark we leave on the hearts and minds of others, the values we pass on to future generations and the positive change we create to inspire the world. In retirement, individuals have the opportunity to reflect on their life's work and consider how they want to be remembered: the opportunity to leave a legacy that reflects their values, passions and aspirations.

Identify Your Values

The first step to building a legacy is to identify your values, the core beliefs and principles that guide your actions and shape your decisions. Whether it's integrity, compassion, or commitment to social justice, your values serve as the foundation of your legacy, providing a roadmap for the impact you want to create on the world.

In retirement, individuals have the opportunity to reflect on their values and consider how they want to express them in their legacy. Whether through philanthropy, volunteering or advocacy, retirees can leverage their values to create positive change in the world and leave a legacy that reflects their beliefs and their deepest aspirations.

Make Differences

One of the most effective ways to build a legacy in retirement is to make a difference: by contributing to the problem, advocating for positive change and making the world better than it already was. Whether it's volunteering at a local charity, supporting environmental conservation or mentoring youth in your community, retirees have opportunities to put their time, resources and experience to good use and utilize their abilities and resources to create positive change in the world.

However, making a difference in retirement provides benefits beyond personal satisfaction: it fosters a sense of connection, belonging and purpose that enriches every aspect of life. By contributing to those important causes, retirees can enjoy a sense of fulfilment and satisfaction, filling every moment of their later years with joy, vitality and meaning.

Passing on Wisdom

Another important aspect of building a retirement legacy is passing on wisdom – sharing the lessons learned and experiences gained throughout life with future generations. Whether through storytelling, mentoring or teaching, retirees have the opportunity to pass on their knowledge and wisdom to others, inspiring them to learn, grow and succeed in life.

Additionally, passing on wisdom by retirees brings benefits beyond personal satisfaction: it fosters a sense of connection and continuity between generations, ensuring that the lessons of the past are not forgotten. Thus, future generations have the necessary tools to meet life's challenges with ease, courage and tenacity.

Create a Lasting Impact

Ultimately, building a retirement legacy is about creating a lasting impact, a testament to your impact on the world and the lives you've touched along the way. Whether through philanthropy, volunteerism or advocacy, retirees have the opportunity to leave a legacy that will last for generations to come: a legacy of love, kindness, compassion and positive change.

Moreover, making a lasting impact in retirement offers benefits beyond personal satisfaction: it fosters a sense of immortality, knowing that your contributions will live on long after you're gone. By building a retirement legacy, retirees can tap into a sense of purpose and significance that transcends boundaries of time and space, leaving a mark on the world that will last for generations to come.

Conclusion

In short, "Legacy Building" is a celebration of the transformative potential of retirement to create a lasting impact in the world. Whether you are making a difference, imparting wisdom or creating a lasting impact, retirement offers the opportunity to build a legacy that reflects your values, passions and aspirations. In the Retirement Renaissance, the journey to build a legacy is not just about leaving a mark on the world: it is about finding fulfilment, purpose and meaning in shaping the future of generations to come.

Part IV:
Wellness and Well-being

Retirement is not just a time to focus on financial planning and leisure activities; it's also an opportunity to prioritize health, wellness and overall happiness. In this section, 'Wellness and Wellbeing', we explore the importance of looking after oneself in retirement, highlighting strategies and practices that can improve the physical, mental and emotional health, while helping to create a rich and meaningful retirement experience.

Bringing Comprehensive Health

Happiness in retirement goes beyond physical health: it includes a holistic approach to happiness that includes the mental, emotional, social and spiritual aspects of life. In retirement, individuals have the opportunity to prioritize self-care, engage in activities that bring joy and satisfaction and foster a sense of balance and harmony in life.

Additionally, comprehensive health care in retirement offers benefits beyond just feeling good: it can also improve quality of life, promote longevity and contribute to a sense of well-being, vitality and purpose in life in the years to come. By taking care of themselves, mentally and physically, retirees can lay the foundation for a rewarding and meaningful retirement experience.

Prioritize Physical Health

Physical health is the foundation of happiness in retirement, helping individuals remain active, independent and engaged in the world around them. In retirement, individuals have the opportunity to prioritize regular exercise, healthy eating and preventative health measures that can improve physical health and enhance longevity.

Additionally, staying physically active in retirement offers benefits beyond physical health: it can also improve mood, reduce stress and improve cognitive function, contributing to the quality of life i.e. to live better and have a greater sense of happiness. By prioritizing physical health in retirement, individuals can prepare themselves for a vibrant and fulfilling retirement experience.

Enhance Mental and Emotional Health

Mental and emotional health are equally important aspects of well-being in retirement, influencing mood, outlook and overall quality of life. In retirement, individuals have the opportunity to prioritize activities and practices that enhance mental and emotional health, such as mindfulness meditation, relaxation techniques and engaging in hobbies and activities which bring joy and satisfaction. What's more, fostering mental and emotional health in retirement has benefits beyond happiness: it can also improve resilience, reduce the risk of depression and anxiety and improve overall life satisfaction. By taking care of their mental and emotional health, retirees can cultivate an inner sense of peace, balance and resilience, enriching every aspect of their retirement experience.

Promote Social Connection

Social connection is another essential aspect of happiness in retirement, providing support, companionship and a sense of belonging that contributes to overall happiness. In retirement, individuals have the opportunity to prioritize relationships with friends, family, community members and to participate in social activities and events that promote connection and close friendship.

Moreover, fostering social connections in retirement offers benefits beyond just companionship — it can also improve mood, reduce stress and enhance overall life satisfaction. By staying connected with others and cultivating meaningful relationships, retirees can create a support network that enhances their well-being and contributes to a fulfilling and meaningful retirement experience.

Nurturing Mental Health

Mental health is an often over looked aspect of retirement, but it can be a source of deep meaning, purpose and satisfaction later in life. In retirement, individuals have the opportunity to explore their spirituality, connect with themselves and engage in activities that enhance their mental health, such as meditation, prayer, or connection with nature.

Furthermore, nurturing mental health in retirement offers benefits beyond feeling connected: it can also provide a sense of peace, meaning and purpose that enriches every aspect of life. By tapping into their spirituality and connecting to something greater than themselves, retirees can find comfort, guidance and inspiration that enhances their overall health and well-being contributing to a rich and meaningful retirement experience.

Conclusion

In short, 'Wellness and Wellbeing' is a celebration of the importance of self-care in retirement, prioritizing physical, mental, emotional, social and spiritual well-being to create the foundation for a dynamic and fulfilling retirement experience. Whether it's staying physically active, supporting mental and emotional health, promoting social connection, or nurturing mental health, retirees have the opportunity to enjoy total health and wellness. It encourages the person to live a retirement experience that is both fun and meaningful.

In Retirement Renaissance, the journey towards wellness and happiness is not just about feeling good, it is about living life to the fullest, cherishing every moment with gratitude and appreciation and finding satisfaction and purpose in the journey.

Mind, Body, Spirit: Cultivating Holistic Health

Retirement represents a pivotal moment in life: an opportunity not only to enjoy newfound freedom but to prioritize total health of mind, body and spirit. In this chapter, "Mind, Body, Spirit," we explore the connection between these three elements and how nurturing each aspect contributes to a rewarding and purposeful retirement experience.

The Connection of Mind, Body and Spirit

Mind, body and spirit are not isolated entities; rather, they are deeply interconnected aspects of our being, each influencing and shaping the others. In retirement, individuals have the opportunity to recognize and honour this connection, knowing that taking care of one aspect of their health can have a profound impact on others. When the mind is at ease, the body relaxes and the spirit is excited; Conversely, when an aspect of health is neglected, it can affect the overall well-being of the individual. By cultivating total health of mind, body and spirit, retirees can lay the foundation for a vibrant and fulfilling retirement experience.

Nurturing the Mind

The mind is the seat of consciousness, intelligence and creativity; it is the source of our thoughts, emotions and perceptions. In retirement, individuals have the opportunity to nurture their minds through practices such as mindfulness meditation, cognitive stimulation and lifelong learning. What's more, nurturing your mind in retirement has benefits beyond just mental sharpness: it can also improve mood, reduce stress and increase overall life satisfaction. By prioritizing mental health and well-being, retirees can cultivate clarity, focus and resilience to enrich every aspect of their retirement experience.

Honouring the Body

The body is the vessel through which we experience the world: it is the vehicle for our actions, feelings and experiences. In retirement, individuals have the opportunity to honour their bodies through activities such as regular exercise, healthy eating and preventative health care. Additionally, honouring your body in retirement has benefits beyond just physical health: it can also improve mood, increase energy levels and improve overall quality of life. By prioritizing physical health and mental well-being, retirees can foster a sense of vitality, strength and resilience so they can fully enjoy their retirement years.

Spiritual Nourishment

The mind is the essence of who we are: it is the source of our inner wisdom, intuition and connection to something greater than ourselves. In retirement, individuals have the opportunity to nurture their spirit through activities such as meditation, prayer and connecting with nature. What's more, cultivating spirituality in retirement has benefits beyond feeling connected: it can also provide a sense of peace, meaning and purpose that enriches every aspect of life. By tapping into their spirituality and connecting to something greater than themselves, retirees can find comfort, guidance and inspiration that enhances their overall health and well-being, contributing to a rich and meaningful retirement experience.

Cultivate Comprehensive Health

Cultivating holistic health in retirement goes beyond addressing individual symptoms or concerns: it's about recognizing the connection between mind, body and soul and nurturing each aspect to create a feeling of balance, harmony and completeness. Whether through mindfulness meditation, regular exercise or spiritual practice, retirees have the opportunity to cultivate holistic health and enjoy a retirement experience that is both fun and meaningful.

Conclusion

In short, "Mind, Body, Spirit" is a celebration of the connection between these three aspects of our being and the importance of nurturing each to create a foundation for the retirement experience. Whether it's nurturing the mind, honouring the body, or nourishing the spirit, retirees have the opportunity to cultivate holistic wellness and cherish every moment of their retirement journey with gratitude, appreciation and determination. In Retirement Renaissance, the journey to holistic health is not just about feeling good, it's about living life to the fullest, embracing all aspects of who we are and finding fulfilment and purpose on that journey.

Staying Active: Fitness and Recreation in Later Life

Retirement is not the time to slow down; it's an opportunity to stay active, engaged and energised. In this chapter, "Staying Active," we dive deeper into the importance of exercise and recreation in our later life, exploring how staying active can improve physical, mental and emotional health and what the overall quality of life is like in retirement.

The Importance of Staying Active

Staying active is important to maintain health and vitality later in life. Regular physical activity is linked to countless health benefits, including improved cardiovascular health, reduced risk of chronic diseases such as diabetes and hypertension and improved mood, function and cognitive ability.

In retirement, individuals have the opportunity to prioritize physical activity and incorporate it into their daily routine. Whether through structured exercise programs, recreational sports or outdoor activities, staying active can help retirees maintain independence, mobility and overall health.

Physical Health Benefits

Regular exercise has many benefits for retirees' physical health. Engaging in activities such as walking, swimming or cycling can improve cardiovascular health, strengthen muscles and bones and increase flexibility and balance, important factors in preventing falls and maintain mobility later in life.

Additionally, staying active can help control weight, reduce the risk of obesity and improve overall energy levels and endurance, allowing retirees to enjoy better quality of life and physical fitness.

Mental and Emotional Health

In addition to physical health benefits, staying active also provides important mental and emotional benefits for retirees. Exercise has been shown to reduce symptoms of anxiety and depression, improve mood and cognitive function, which are important factors for maintaining mental sharpness and emotional well-being in our later life.

Additionally, participating in recreational activities and hobbies can provide a sense of purpose, fulfilment and joy, contributing to overall life satisfaction and happiness. Whether it's golf, gardening or dancing, staying active can help retirees stay socially connected, engaged and fulfilled during retirement.

Social Connections

Staying active in retirement also provides opportunities for social interaction and connection, an essential aspect of overall well-being. Signing up for group fitness classes, participating in sports tournaments, or participating in community events and activities can help retirees connect with others, build friendships and combat feelings of isolation and loneliness.

Additionally, social connections have been shown to have a positive impact on health and longevity, reduce the risk of chronic diseases and improve overall quality of life. By staying active and participating in social activities, retirees can foster a sense of belonging and community that improves their overall health and contributes to their retirement experience.

Tips for Staying Active

For retirees who want to stay active later in life, there are many options to consider. From low-impact activities like yoga and tai chi to more vigorous activities like hiking and swimming, there's something for everyone.

Additionally, it's important to find activities that are enjoyable and sustainable, as this will increase the likelihood of sticking with them for long term. Whether it's walking with friends, joining group fitness classes or exploring new hobbies and interests, staying active will be a fun and rewarding experience that improves your overall health and quality of life in retirement.

Conclusion

In short, "Staying Active" is a celebration of the importance of fitness and recreation in later life. Whether you take a walk in the park, play tennis with friends, or take up a new hobby, staying active can improve your physical and mental health and overall quality of life in retirement.

In the Retirement Renaissance, staying active doesn't just mean staying healthy: it's about enjoying life to the fullest, staying engaged, vibrant and finding joy and fulfilment being satisfied in every moment. By prioritizing physical activity and staying active in later life, retirees can enjoy a better quality of life and have a retirement experience that is both enriching and meaningful.

Embracing Mindfulness: Finding Peace and Presence

Retirement offers a unique opportunity to slow down, reflect and enjoy the present moment. In this "Embracing Mindfulness" chapter, we explore the transformative power of mindfulness later in life, emphasizing how cultivating awareness and presence can improve happiness, reduce stress and promote a deeper sense of peace and satisfaction in retirement.

Understanding Mindfulness

Mindfulness is the practice of paying attention to the present moment with openness, curiosity and acceptance. It involves being aware of our thoughts, emotions and feelings without judgment, allowing us to experience life more fully and authentically. In retirement, individuals have the opportunity to embrace mindfulness as a way of being, a way of approaching each moment with intention and presence. By cultivating mindfulness, retirees can learn to let go of past regrets and worries about the future and instead focus on what's happening right now.

Benefits of Mindfulness

The benefits of mindfulness are many and include physical, mental and emotional health. Research has shown that practicing mindfulness can reduce stress, anxiety and depression, improve mood, improve cognitive function and boost immune function. Additionally, mindfulness can also improve relationships, increase resilience and foster a greater sense of connection and compassion for yourself and others. By cultivating mindfulness, individuals can create the foundation for a more peaceful, joyful and fulfilling retirement experience.

Practicing mindfulness

There are many ways to practice mindfulness in retirement, from formal meditation practices to informal mindfulness exercises that can be applied to everyday life. Mindfulness meditation involves sitting quietly and focusing on your breathing, bodily sensations, or sounds around you, allowing thoughts and emotions to come and go without getting caught up in them.

Additionally, informal mindfulness practices such as walking, eating, or even washing dishes mindfully can help foster presence and awareness in daily activities. By bringing mindfulness into everyday moments, retirees can infuse their lives with a sense of wonder, gratitude and appreciation for the richness of each moment.

Accept Impermanence

One of the important lessons of mindfulness is to recognize impermanence, which means understanding that everything in life is constantly changing and ephemeral. In retirement, individuals have the opportunity to accept impermanence as a natural part of the human experience and find beauty and meaning in life's fleeting moments. By cultivating mindfulness, retirees can learn to let go of attachment to the past and fear of the future and embrace the present moment with openness and curiosity. In doing so, they can experience a deeper sense of peace, acceptance and gratitude for the precious gift of life.

Finding Peace and Presence

Ultimately, applying mindfulness in retirement is about finding peace and being present in each moment, regardless of external circumstances or conditions. By cultivating awareness and acceptance of the present moment, retirees can experience life more fully and authentically and find joy and satisfaction in the simple pleasures of our daily life

In addition, mindfulness can also serve as a powerful tool for dealing with inevitable challenges and transitions in later life, providing a source of strength, resilience and equanimity in inner peace when faced with adversity. By adopting mindfulness as a way of being, retirees can create a retirement experience characterized by a deep sense of peace, presence and meaning.

Conclusion

In short, "Embracing Mindfulness" is a celebration of the transformative power of mindfulness in later life. Whether you're meditating quietly, taking a mental walk, in nature, or simply enjoying a cup of tea, mindfulness can improve health, reduce stress and promote a sense of peace and purpose more deeply in retirement.

In the Retirement Renaissance, the journey towards mindfulness is not only about finding peace but also about embracing life fully, with awareness, presence and gratitude for the precious gifts in every moment. By cultivating mindfulness in retirement, individuals can experience a deeper sense of connection to themselves, others and the world around them, while creating a retirement experience characterized by joy, delight, satisfaction and purpose.

Part V:
Navigating Relationships and Nurturing the Soul

Retirement not only marks a transition in professional life but also in relationships. In this section, "Navigating Relationships," we delve deeper into the dynamics of interpersonal relationships in retirement, exploring how to nurture and maintain meaningful relationships, forge new relationships and navigate the complexities of family, friendships and romantic partnerships later in life.

Relationship Dynamics in Retirement

Retirement often brings significant changes in relationships, whether it's spending more time with a spouse, reconnecting with adult children, or forming new friendships in a retirement community mind. Understanding the dynamics of relationships in retirement is essential to navigating this transition with grace and compassion. In retirement, individuals have the opportunity to reassess their relationships, prioritize those that bring them joy and fulfilment and let go of those that no longer serve them.

By promoting open communication, mutual respect and empathy, retirees can create relationships characterized by love, support and understanding.

Maintaining Relationships with Adult Children

For many retirees, retirement coincides with changes in relationships with adult children. As children grow up and start families of their own, retirees may find themselves facing new roles and boundaries in their family dynamic. In retirement, individuals have the opportunity to nurture and maintain relationships with their adult children by promoting open communication, respecting their autonomy and offering support and advice when necessary. By cultivating strong, healthy relationships with their adult children, retirees can create a sense of continuity and connection that enriches every aspect of their retirement experience.

Nurturing Friendships

Friendships are an important source of support, camaraderie and joy in retirement. Whether it's reconnecting with old friends or making new connections in a retirement community, nurturing friendships is an important aspect of managing relationships later in life.

In retirement, individuals have the opportunity to prioritize friendships that bring them joy and fulfilment, invest time and energy to nurture those connections and let go of friendships that no longer serve them too. By surrounding themselves with positive, supportive friends, retirees can create a sense of community and belonging to improve their overall health and quality of life.

Navigating Romantic Relationships

Romantic relationships can also undergo significant changes in retirement, as couples navigate the transition from work to retirement together. Whether it's spending more time together, exploring new hobbies and interests or renegotiating roles and responsibilities, managing romantic relationships in retirement requires open communication, openness, compromise and mutual respect.

In retirement, individuals have the opportunity to deepen their relationship with their partner, rekindle passion and intimacy and create a shared vision for the future. By prioritizing quality time together, expressing appreciation, affection and nurturing the emotional connection between them, retirees can create a romantic relationship characterized by affection, love, companionship and mutual support.

Community Building

Finally, building community is an important aspect of managing relationships in retirement. Whether it's joining a club or organization, participating in volunteer activities, or attending social events at retirement communities, building a community provides opportunities to connect, bond and close friendship.

In retirement, individuals have the opportunity to cultivate relationships with like-minded people who share their interests, values and passions. By actively participating in community activities and fostering connections with others, retirees can create a sense of belonging and purpose that enriches every aspect of their retirement experience.

Conclusion

In short, "Navigating Relationships" is a celebration of the importance of interpersonal connection in retirement. Whether it's nurturing relationships with adult children, cultivating friendships, forming romantic partnerships or building community, relationships are an important source of support, companionship and joy.

In the Retirement Renaissance, the relationship journey is not just about maintaining connections but also about cultivating meaningful affiliations that bring joy, fulfilment and purpose to every aspect of life. By prioritizing open communication, mutual respect and empathy, retirees can create relationships characterized by love, support and understanding and create a retirement experience that is both a fun and meaningful.

Family Dynamics: Redefining Roles and Relationships

Retirement is not just a personal milestone; this is a significant change that can reshape family dynamics and relationships. In this chapter, "Family Dynamics," we explore the complexities of navigating family relationships in retirement, examining how roles and relationships develop and how individuals can form strong, supportive family bonds while rediscovering life, passion and purpose later in life.

Roles in the Transformation Process

Retirement often marks a transition of roles within the family unit. For many retirees, the transition from a life focused on career to one focused on leisure and personal activities can lead to changes in how they view themselves and their position.

Adult children may find themselves taking on more caregiving or financial support responsibilities, while retirees may struggle to redefine their identities outside of work. Understanding and managing these changing roles is critical to maintaining harmony and balance in family dynamics.

Stay Connected

One of the main challenges of family dynamics in retirement is staying connected and communicating with adult children and other family members. As children grow up and start their own families, retirees may find themselves struggling with feelings of loneliness or isolation. In retirement, individuals have the opportunity to prioritize quality time with family members, whether through regular visits, phone calls or virtual meetings.

By promoting open communication and expressing love and support, retirees can strengthen family bonds and create a sense of connection and belonging, enriching the retirement experience.

Support for Adult Children

Retirement can also lead to changes in the relationship between parents and adult children, including support and guidance. As children face the challenges of adulthood, retirees may find themselves offering advice, financial help or emotional support. In retirement, individuals have the opportunity to support their adult children's efforts while establishing healthy boundaries and fostering their independence. By providing advice and encouragement while respecting their autonomy, retirees can create a supportive environment that allows their adult children to thrive.

Navigating Intergenerational Relationships

Intergenerational relationships play an important role in family dynamics in retirement. Whether bonding with grandchildren, sharing stories and wisdom with young relatives or bridging the generation gap through shared activities and experiences, intergenerational connections can enrich the lives of retirees and their families.

In retirement, individuals have the opportunity to maintain strong, meaningful relationships with younger generations by actively participating in family activities, creating opportunities for bonding and connection and act as a role model and mentor. By nurturing these intergenerational relationships, retirees can create a sense of continuity and connection that transcends age and strengthen family bonds.

Conflict Resolution

Finally, managing family dynamics in retirement may also involve managing conflicts or tensions that arise within the family unit. Whether it's disagreements about caregiving responsibilities, financial decisions or lifestyle choices, conflict can strain relationships and create stress for retirees and their families.

In retirement, individuals have the opportunity to approach conflict with compassion, empathy and understanding, seeking to resolve differences through open communication and compromise. By cultivating a culture of mutual respect and support within the family, retirees can resolve conflicts constructively and thereby strengthen their relationships.

Conclusion

In short, "Family Dynamics" reflects the development of roles and relationships within the family unit upon retirement. Whether it's switching roles, staying connected, supporting adult children, nurturing intergenerational relationships, or resolving conflict, navigating family dynamics requires teamwork. Empathy, communication and commitment foster strong, supportive relationships.

In the Retirement Renaissance, the journey of family dynamics isn't just about navigating change: it's about seizing opportunities to strengthen connections, foster understanding and enrich every aspect of life. By prioritizing open communication, empathy and respect, retirees can navigate family dynamics with grace and compassion, while creating a retirement experience characterized by love, connection and purpose.

Social Connections: Building and Maintaining Friendships

Retirement is not just a phase of life spent in solitude; it is an opportunity to form meaningful social connections and form friendships that enrich our lives. In this chapter, "Social Connections," we explore the importance of forming and maintaining friendships later in life, highlight the benefits of social interaction and offer strategies for maintaining meaningful relationships in retirement.

The Importance of Social Connection

Social connection is essential for our health, no matter what our age is. In retirement, when the transition can lead to changes in habits and social circles, the importance of maintaining friendships becomes even more apparent. Research consistently shows that strong social connections are linked to better physical and mental health outcomes, including reduced risk of depression, anxiety and cognitive decline. In addition, friendship provides emotional support, companionship and a sense of belonging, important factors that help us overcome life's challenges and find joy and fulfilment in the later years of our lives. By prioritizing social connections, retirees can create a support network that improves their overall health and enriches their retirement experience.

Build New Friendships

Retirement offers a unique opportunity to form new friendships and expand our social circles. Whether it's joining clubs or interest groups, volunteering in the community, or attending social events and gatherings, retirees have plenty of opportunities to meet new people and establish connections based on shared interests and values.

Additionally, technology makes it easier than ever to connect with others, allowing retirees to join online communities, attend virtual events and stay connected with friends and associates, family members, regardless of circumstances or geographical distance. By embracing new experiences and stepping out of their comfort zone, retirees can open themselves up to a world of possibilities for forming new friendships and enriching their social lives.

Maintain Existing Friendships

While forming new friendships is important, nurturing and maintaining existing relationships in retirement is equally important. Long-term friendships are a source of comfort, support and joy, and investing time and energy in these relationships can strengthen bonds and deepen connections over time. In retirement, individuals have the opportunity to prioritize quality time with friends, whether through regular phone calls, video chats or in-person meetings. Planning outings, sharing meals and participating in activities together can help maintain connections and create lasting memories that maintain friendships for years to come.

Navigating Changes in Social Circles

Retirement often brings changes in social circles as colleagues retire, family members move away and interests and priorities change. Coping with these changes can be challenging, but it also offers an opportunity to reassess our social networks and nurture relationships that align with our values and retirement aspirations. In retirement, individuals may seek new means and social opportunities to connect, whether through community organizations, religious groups or online communities. By embracing change and staying open to new experiences, retirees can continue to form and maintain social connections that bring joy, satisfaction and meaning to their lives.

Prioritize Quality Over Quantity

To form and maintain friendships in retirement, it's important to prioritize quality over quantity. While having a large social network can be beneficial, it's the depth and authenticity of our relationships that really matter. Investing time and energy in cultivating meaningful relationships with a few close friends can bring more satisfaction and support than superficial interactions with many acquaintances.

Additionally, focusing on quality friendships allows retirees to cultivate relationships based on mutual respect, trust and understanding, essential to weathering life's ups and downs, with grace and resilience. By focusing on quality over quantity, retirees can create a social circle that enriches their lives and improves their overall health in retirement.

Conclusion

In short, "Social Connections" is a celebration of the importance of forming and maintaining friendships later in life. Whether forming new connections, nurturing existing relationships or navigating changes in social circles, social connections are an important source of support, friendship and joy in retirement.

In the Retirement Renaissance, the journey of social connection is not just about filling our social calendars but also about cultivating meaningful relationships that bring depth and richness to our lives.

By prioritizing social connections and investing in quality friendships, retirees can create a support network that improves their well-being, enriches their retirement experience and helps them rediscover their passion and purpose in later life.

The Importance of Prayer: Nurturing the Soul in Later Life

In the hustle and bustle of our daily lives, it's easy to overlook the power of prayer, a timeless practice that has been a source of comfort, strength and spiritual connection for countless generations. However, as we navigate the complexities of retirement and seek to rediscover passion and purpose later in life, prayer takes on new meaning: a beacon of hope and direction to light the way forward for us.

Find Comfort in Calm

Retirement often brings a new sense of freedom and flexibility - the opportunity to slow down, reflect and enjoy quiet moments that may have eluded us during our working years. In these quiet moments, prayer offers refuge: a refuge from the noise and distractions of the world and a chance to connect with something greater than ourselves. Whether through formal prayer rituals, silent meditation, or simply communing with nature, prayer provides a space for introspection, contemplation and spiritual renewal. This allows us to quiet our minds, open our hearts and tap into the deepest truths and wisdom that lies within us - all essential elements of the retreat journey of rebirth.

Unleash your Strength in Times of Uncertainty

Retirement can be a time of transition and uncertainty, one marked by changes in habits, identity and purpose. In these uncertain times, prayer is a source of strength and resilience, a reminder that we are not alone on this journey and that there is a higher power guiding us through the ups and downs and depression of life. Through prayer, we can express our fears, doubts and concerns, knowing that we are heard and held in the loving embrace of God's grace. It allows us to unburden ourselves, release attachments and trust in God's plan for life - a profound act of faith that sustains us through the challenges and uncertainties of retirement.

Cultivate Gratitude and Perspective

Amid life's trials and tribulations, prayer invites us to cultivate an attitude of gratitude and perspective: to count our blessings, recognize the gifts around us and find beauty in our simplest moments. It is the practice of mindfulness and awareness that allows us to appreciate the richness and magnificence of life, even in the face of adversity. In retirement, prayer provides an opportunity to reflect on the journey we have been on, the lessons we have learned and the blessings we have received along the way. It invites us to celebrate the joys, honour the sorrows and embrace the fullness of the human experience with humility and grace.

Foster connection and community

Prayer is not just a personal practice, it is also a communal experience that fosters connection and solidarity between like-minded souls. Whether it is group worship, spiritual gatherings or sharing prayers with loved ones, prayer brings people together in a spirit of fellowship and solidarity, reminding us that we all are interconnected and interdependent on this life journey.

In retirement, prayer offers the opportunity to nurture meaningful connections with others who share our values, beliefs and aspirations. This allows us to support and encourage one another, offer words of encouragement and comfort and draw strength from the collective wisdom and grace of our community.

Embrace the Sacredness of Life

Ultimately, prayer is about celebrating the sacredness of life - the acknowledgment of God's presence that permeates every aspect of our existence and gives it meaning and purpose. In retirement, prayer invites us to embrace the sacredness of each moment, honour the inherent dignity and worth of every living thing and live with respect, compassion and love. As we embark on the journey of retirement revival, let us embrace the transformative power of prayer: nourishing the soul, finding strength in times of uncertainty, cultivating knowing grace and perspective, foster connection and community and embrace the sacredness of life in all its aspects, beauty and complexity. For, in prayer we discover the true nature of who we are and we awaken the infinite possibilities that lie within us.

Part VI:
Financial Freedom and Security

Retirement is not just a phase of life to enjoy; This is also the time to ensure financial stability and security for the future. In this section of "Financial Freedom and Security," we explore the importance of financial planning, investment strategies and prudent lifestyle choices in retirement, helping individuals achieve prosperity, financial independence and peace of mind later in life.

The Importance of Financial Freedom

Financial freedom is the foundation of a fulfilling retirement experience. It provides individuals with the flexibility and autonomy to pursue their passions, explore new interests and enjoy a comfortable lifestyle without the burden of stress or financial instability. In retirement, individuals have the opportunity to evaluate their financial situation, set clear goals, priorities and develop a plan to achieve financial freedom. By making wise decisions and taking proactive steps to manage their finances, retirees can create a solid foundation for a secure and prosperous retirement.

Plan Your Finances Carefully

Careful financial planning is essential to achieving financial freedom and security in retirement. This involves assessing current financial resources, estimating future costs and developing a comprehensive plan to effectively manage income, expenses and investments. In retirement, individuals may need to consider many different factors when planning their finances, including sources of retirement income such as pensions and retirement savings accounts as well as expenses, health care costs, taxes and inflation. By working with a financial advisor and developing a personalized financial plan, retirees can ensure their finances are aligned with their retirement goals and priorities.

Investment Strategy

Investment strategy plays an important role in achieving financial freedom and retirement security. Retirees need to balance capital preservation with income generation to maintain their lifestyle over the long term. In retirement, individuals may need to adjust their investment strategies to reflect changing risk tolerance, income needs and time horizons. This may involve diversifying investments across different asset classes, rebalancing the portfolio regularly and exploring income-generating strategies such as stocks, bonds, annuities and dividend payment.

Lifestyle Choices

Lifestyle choices also play an important role in achieving financial freedom and retirement security. Retirees may need to adjust their spending habits, living arrangements and leisure activities to fit their financial goals and priorities. In retirement, individuals have the opportunity to reassess their priorities, downsize their living space and explore cost-effective ways to enjoy their retirement years. By adopting a frugal mindset, prioritizing experiences over material possessions and adopting a minimalist lifestyle, retirees can further expand their retirement savings and achieve financial security.

Realize Financial Independence

Ultimately, achieving financial freedom and retirement security isn't just about accumulating wealth: it's about embracing financial independence and living life on your terms. It's the confidence and peace of mind to pursue your passions, explore new opportunities and enjoy a rewarding retirement experience without financial constraints.

In the Retirement Renaissance, the journey towards financial freedom and security is not just about achieving a specific financial milestone: it is also about creating a sense of empowerment and autonomy that allows individuals to live their life to the fullest with confidence and determination. By prioritizing financial planning, investment strategies and prudent lifestyle choices, retirees can achieve financial independence and create a retirement experience characterized by freedom, security and choice.

Conclusion

In short, "Financial Freedom and Security" celebrates the importance of financial planning, investment strategies and prudent lifestyle choices to achieve a secure and prosperous retirement. Whether it's evaluating their financial resources, developing a personal financial plan or adopting a savings mindset, retirees have the opportunity to achieve financial independence and enjoy their vacation experience. Retirement is characterized by freedom, security and peace of mind.

Financial Planning for the Future: Strategies for Long-Term Security

Retirement marks an important milestone in life, marking the transition from a career-focused existence to a period of relaxation, exploration and fulfilment. However, to truly grasp the possibilities of this new phase, planning for long-term financial security is essential. In this chapter, "Financial Planning for the Future," we explore the strategies and considerations needed to ensure a stable and prosperous retirement journey.

Understand the Importance of Financial Planning

Financial planning is the foundation for building a secure retirement fund. This involves assessing a person's current financial situation, setting achievable goals and developing a comprehensive roadmap for managing income, expenses, investments and retirement assets. In the Retirement Renaissance, financial planning is about more than accumulating wealth: it's about creating a framework that allows individuals to live life on their own terms, unconstrained by worry or financial instability. By taking proactive steps to plan for the future, retirees can have peace of mind and confidence in their financial abilities.

Set Realistic Goals

The first step to effective financial planning is to set realistic and achievable goals for the future. This may include estimating retirement costs, determining desired lifestyle choices and identifying sources of income such as pensions, social security and retirement savings accounts. In retirement, individuals have the opportunity to reassess their priorities and align their financial goals with their personal values and aspirations. Whether it's traveling the world, pursuing hobbies and interests, or leaving a legacy for future generations, setting clear and achievable goals is essential.

Diversification and Asset Allocation

Diversification and asset allocation are fundamentals of investment management that play an important role in achieving long-term financial security in retirement. Diversification involves spreading investments across different asset classes, such as stocks, bonds, real estate and alternative investments, to minimize risk and improve returns. In retirement, individuals may need to rebalance their portfolios to reflect their changing risk tolerance, time horizon and income needs. By diversifying their investments and maintaining a balanced portfolio, retirees can minimize the impact of market fluctuations and ensure a steady stream of income to support their future lifestyle.

Managing Retirement Income

Managing retirement income is another important aspect of financial planning for the future. Retirees need to consider how to optimize their income stream to meet their financial needs while preserving their long-term capital. In retirement, individuals can withdraw income from a variety of sources, including pensions, social security, retirement savings accounts, and investment portfolios. By developing a sustainable withdrawal strategy, retirees can ensure they have enough income to cover expenses while protecting themselves against the risk of running out of savings.

Make an Emergency Plan

Contingency planning is an essential part of financial planning for the future because it helps retirees prepare for unexpected events and uncertainties that may arise in the future. This may include planning for health care costs, long-term care needs or unexpected changes in financial situation.

In retirement, individuals have the opportunity to explore options such as long-term care insurance, health savings accounts and estate planning strategies to protect their assets and ensure a secure future for yourself and for your loved ones. By taking proactive steps to plan for the unexpected, retirees can face life's uncertainties with confidence and peace of mind.

Conclusion

In short, "Financial Planning for the Future" is the roadmap to achieving long-term security and prosperity in retirement. Whether it's setting realistic goals, diversifying investments, managing retirement income or effective financial planning, the unexpected is essential to creating a retirement experience characterized by freedom, security and peace of mind.

In the Retirement Renaissance, the financial planning journey is not just about accumulating wealth: it is about creating a sense of empowerment and self-reliance, allowing individuals to live life to the fullest with confidence and determination. By prioritizing financial planning and taking proactive steps to secure their financial future, retirees can embark on a retirement journey filled with promise, possibility and fulfilment.

Estate Planning and Legacy Management: Ensuring Your Wishes are Honoured

As retirees begin the journey of rediscovering passion and purpose later in life, it is important to address estate planning and estate management issues. In this chapter, "Estate Planning and Legacy Management," we dive deeper into the importance of preparing for the future, ensuring one's wishes are respected and leaving a legacy lasting for future generations.

Understanding Estate Planning

Estate planning involves making decisions about how to manage and distribute a person's assets and affairs in the event of incapacity or death. While this may not be the most exciting topic to discuss, estate planning is essential for protecting a person's financial interests, ensuring their loved ones are cared for and minimizing litigation as well as complications after their death. In retirement, individuals have the opportunity to create a comprehensive estate plan that reflects their values, priorities and desires for the future. This may include writing a will, establishing trusts, naming beneficiaries for retirement accounts and insurance policies and preparing advance health care directives and final dispositions.

Protect Your Inheritance

Wealth management goes beyond the simple distribution of assets: it is about preserving people's values, beliefs and memories for future generations. In retirement, individuals have the opportunity to reflect on their life journey, determine what is most important to them and take proactive steps to ensure their legacy lives on long after they have retired. This may involve recording family history and stories, passing on treasured legacies and traditions, and planning charitable donations or philanthropic efforts. By securing their inheritance, retirees can leave an important mark on the world and inspire future generations to continue their values and ideals.

Navigating the Complexity

Estate planning and asset management can be complex and nuanced processes, requiring careful consideration of legal, financial and emotional factors. In retirement, individuals may need to work with a team of professionals, including estate planning attorneys, financial advisors and tax experts, to develop a plan that meets their needs and goals.

Additionally, estate planning laws and regulations can vary by jurisdiction, making it important for retirees to stay up to date with changes that may affect their estate plans. By taking a proactive, comprehensive approach to estate planning, retirees can confidently navigate complex issues and ensure their wishes are respected.

Facilitate Family Communication

Effective estate planning also involves facilitating open and honest communication with family members about their wishes and intentions. In retirement, individuals have the opportunity to engage in meaningful conversations with loved ones about their estate plans, clarify their expectations, address their concerns and foster a sense of solidarity and understanding. By involving family members in the estate planning process, retirees can reduce the risk of litigation and long-term conflict and ensure that their wishes are carried out as intended.

Additionally, family communication can strengthen relationships and create a sense of shared purpose and responsibility in preserving the family legacy.

Embrace the future

In short, "Estate Planning and Legacy Management" is a call to action for retirees to take charge of their future and ensure their wishes are fulfilled. Whether it's drafting a will, securing your inheritance, managing complex matters or facilitating family communication, estate planning is an essential part of your business. Retirement planning allows individuals to leave a meaningful legacy for future generations.

In the Retirement Renaissance, the estate planning journey isn't just about preparing for the inevitable: it's about looking to the future with confidence and peace of mind, knowing that your wishes will be fulfilled. respected and the legacy will live on. By prioritizing estate planning and legacy management, retirees can create a retirement experience characterized by security, fulfilment and a sense of lasting impact on the world.

Conclusion: Embracing Your Retirement Renaissance Journey

As we come to the conclusion of "Retirement Renaissance: Rediscovering Passion and Purpose in Later Life," it's time to reflect on the journey we've taken together. Throughout this book, we explore the countless opportunities and challenges that retirement brings and discover the secrets to unlocking a life filled with passion, purpose and fulfilment.

Accept Changes

Retirement is a time of transition, a time when we let go of the familiar habits and identities of our working lives and embrace new possibilities and opportunities for growth. It's an opportunity to redefine ourselves, explore our passions and interests and chart a path for the future that aligns with our values and aspirations.

In the Retirement Renaissance, change is not something to fear or resist; it is something to be welcomed and celebrated as a natural part of the journey towards a more fulfilling and meaningful life. By embracing change with open hearts and minds, retirees can explore new horizons, form new relationships and fulfil their potential later in life.

Rediscover Passion and Purpose

At the heart of Retirement Renaissance is the idea of rediscovering passion and purpose later in life. Retirement is not a time to rest on our laurels but a time to rekindle the flame of passion that may have dimmed over the years and pursue our deepest desires with renewed vigour and enthusiasm. Whether it's exploring new hobbies and interests, pursuing creative projects or giving back to the community through volunteering and philanthropy, retirees have the opportunity to tap into their passions and create a life rich in meaning and fulfilment. By embracing our passions and aligning our actions with a sense of purpose, we can tap into the true potential of our retirement years and experience a new sense of vitality and joy.

Create Meaningful Connections

Throughout our retirement journey, we discovered the importance of establishing and maintaining meaningful relationships with others. Whether they are family, friends, retirees or members of our community, these connections give us support, camaraderie and a sense of belonging, enriching us in every aspect of our lives.

In today's Retirement Renaissance, creating meaningful connections is not just about expanding our social circles but also about cultivating deep, authentic relationships that nourish the mind, our souls and bring us closer to those who always hold us closer in their hearts. By prioritizing relationships and community, retirees can create a support network that helps them through life's ups and downs and ensures they never have to travel alone.

Living with Gratitude and Resilience

As we face the challenges and uncertainties of retirement, it is important to cultivate a mindset of gratitude and resilience to help us weather life's storms with grace and dignity. Gratitude reminds us to appreciate the blessings that surround us every day: enjoy simple pleasures, cherish moments of joy and find beauty in the world around us.

Likewise, resilience teaches us to bounce back from setbacks and adversity, embrace change with courage and resilience and see challenges as opportunities to grow and transform. By living with gratitude and resilience, retirees can navigate the challenges of retirement with confidence and grace, knowing they have the strength and resilience to overcome any obstacle or afraid of things happening on their way.

Seize your retirement renaissance

As we say goodbye to "Retirement Renaissance: Rediscovering Passion and Purpose in Later Life," I invite you to embrace your own retirement revival journey with open arms and an open heart. Whether you're just starting your retirement journey or are already well on your way, remember that the best is yet to come. Embrace change with courage and curiosity. Rediscover your passions and pursue them with enthusiasm. Build meaningful connections with others and cherish the moments of joy and laughter you share.

Live with gratitude and resilience, knowing that every day is a gift and an opportunity to create the life you've always dreamed of. In the Retirement Renaissance, the journey is yours and the possibilities are endless. So move forward with confidence and enthusiasm, and let your retirement be a testament to the power of passion, purpose and possibilities later in life. Your best days are still ahead, so grab them with both hands and make the most of every moment. Embrace the rebirth of your retirement and let it be the beginning of the most special chapter of your life.

About the Author

In the tapestry of life, each thread weaves a unique story and Anupam Pandey is a visionary writer with a keen talent for crafting stories of self-development in the vibrant colours of diverse experiences. With a background in mechanical engineering, Anupam's journey has traversed the realms of science, professional pursuits and a deep passion for empowering others through the written word.

Academic Foundations: A Mechanical Engineer's Journey

Anupam Pandey's academic journey began in the fascinating world of mechanical engineering. His curiosity to understand the intricacies of the physical world led him to delve deep into the intricacies of machines and systems. The rigorous discipline of engineering gave him problem-solving skills, analytical thinking and a methodical approach to challenges. These skills would later be combined with his passion for writing and self-development. Beyond formulas and blueprints, Anupam's educational journey fostered a mindset of continuous learning and adaptability. These qualities, honed in academia, would become an integral part of his journey as a writer committed to personal transformation and growth.

The Pen as a Catalyst: A Journey into Self-Help

Writing Anupam Pandey's transition from the world of engineering to the field of self-help books was more than just a career change. It was a conscious decision to combine technical acumen with human understanding. His first foray into self-help literature was marked by few powerful works of his, each a testament to his commitment to promoting personal transformation.

In "Frugality: Being Mindful of Your Expenses," Anupam explores the nuances of being mindful of your spending and being financially conscious. This book serves as a practical guide for those seeking financial security and a harmonious relationship with money. Anupam's ability to translate complex financial concepts into easily accessible insights has demonstrated his talent for clarity and relevance.

'"Time Alchemy: Transforming Moments into Success" marked another milestone in Anupam's literary journey. In this book, he reveals his secret to turning moments into stepping stones to success. Drawing on his own experiences and timeless wisdom, Anupam inspired readers to view time not as a constraint, but as a canvas for personal and professional growth.

"Grow Old Gracefully" is his third self-help book which is an insightful and empowering book designed to illuminate the path of aging with intentionality, resilience and an unwavering spirit. As we embark on the journey of life's later chapters, this comprehensive guide serves as a beacon, offering practical wisdom, inspiring narratives and actionable strategies to navigate the aging process with grace

"Forgiveness and Healing: Letting Go of the Past for a Brighter Future", is a magnum opus that reflects his evolution as a writer and advocate of personal growth. More than just a collection of words, this book is a deep exploration of the transformative power of forgiveness. Anupam takes readers on a journey of self-discovery and healing through insightful stories, practical tools and compassionate guidance.

His unique writing style, which combines wisdom and approachability, resonates with readers of all backgrounds. Anupam Pandey's literary endeavours go beyond traditional self-help. They embody a genuine desire to encourage, inspire and empower others on their unique journey of personal transformation.

Beyond the Pages: Anupam Pandey as a Thought Leader

Anupam's influence extends beyond the pages of his books. As a thought leader in the personal development field, he engages with audiences across multiple platforms, sharing insights and fostering a community dedicated to growth. His ability to connect with people on a personal level, coupled with a genuine passion for their well-being, makes Anupam not just a writer, but also a mentor and guide towards a better future.

Anupam Pandey's life is an intricate thread of technology, writing and self-development that creates a story that reflects authenticity and determination. His commitment to helping people embrace their personal journeys is not just a job, it's a calling. That mission continues to unfold with every word written and every life touched by the transformative power of his work.

Disclaimer

The information presented in "Retirement Renaissance: Rediscovering Passion and Purpose in Later Life" is intended for general informational purposes only. While every effort has been made to ensure the accuracy and completeness of the content, the author and publisher make no representations or warranties of any kind, express or implied, about the completeness, accuracy, reliability, suitability, or availability with respect to the information contained in this book for any purpose.

The content of this book is not intended to serve as professional advice, including but not limited to financial, legal, medical, or psychological advice. Readers are encouraged to seek the services of qualified professionals in these areas to address their specific needs and circumstances.

The author and publisher disclaim any liability for any loss, injury, or damage incurred as a result of reliance upon the information presented in this book. Readers are solely responsible for their own actions and decisions based on the information provided.

Additionally, any references to specific products, services, or organizations are purely for illustrative purposes and do not imply endorsement or recommendation by the author or publisher.

Readers should use their discretion and judgment when applying the concepts, strategies, and recommendations discussed in this book to their own lives and situations.

By reading "Retirement Renaissance: Rediscovering Passion and Purpose in Later Life," readers acknowledge and agree to these disclaimers and understand that the content is intended to inspire and inform rather than substitute professional advice.

www.ingramcontent.com/pod-product-compliance
Ingram Content Group UK Ltd.
Pitfield, Milton Keynes, MK11 3LW, UK
UKHW020244240426
12048UKWH00026B/1597